How to receive a MIRACLE & retain it

Chris

LoveWorld Publications

How to Receive a Miracle and Retain it
ISBN 978-35623-1-2

First Printing 2001

Copyright © 2001 LoveWorld Publications

All scripture quotations are taken from the King James   Version of the Bible unless otherwise indicated.

BELIEVERS' LOVEWORLD INC.
a.k.a Christ Embassy

UNITED KINGDOM:
Christ Embassy Int'l Office
Suite 219 Estuary House
Ballards Road
Dagenham RM10 9AB

P.O. Box 21520
London E10 5FG
Tel: -208-5172367

NIGERIA:
P.O. Box 13563
Ikeja, Lagos.
Tel: 234-1-4934393

email:cec@christembassy.org
website:www.christembassy.org

Contents

Whatever God says to us is full of living
power
- Prov 4:20 fall they word in heart then keep heal
Matt 12:35 - A good man (e so are going)
NB - good treasure is the word of God
- Could a heart be the word of God is there who
could open the devil opened it I mined it
if all God was off
But even God can stand his word Pr healing
"1 Cor 4:7 we have this treasure in earthen
vessel
The word of God actuates us
- Cherish the word of God It will pull you
in type - up
- good things in everything a saw come
to you if you say well you won't be
set what u don't want to see u
came
The scripture of the world or
deny me to make you a
perpetual slave

- Tithe open the window of heaven
- the moment u get u money late
out the Tithe Dad tell u real
Sunday. Pour u out a Blessing
- "A blessing
- everything you do will be
orientated, empowered
- Psi Rivers of water - anointing
- what were told dwell they
prosper this life big shall not
whether so of the anointing
- man who is u offering

Introduction

A miracle is that supernatural intervention of God that transcends all human reasoning. Everyone at one point or the other requires this supernatural intervention. When we are faced with a seemingly hopeless situation; when we require the circumstances of our lives to change; when medical Science offers little or no hope and human reasoning proffers no solution - it's time for a miracle!

This book contains vital information on basic principles that will help you reach out and receive your miracle, and beyond that, teach you how to ward off the counterattack of the devil, and retain your miracle.

Get Rid of The Wrong Assumptions

Assumptions, opinions and teachings not based on the Word of God have held many from receiving from God. To receive a miracle, therefore, you will have to rid yourself of these limiting assumptions. Some of them even sound religious or pious, but they can only offer human comfort devoid of the assurance of the Holy Spirit.

Assumption 1:

GOD WILL HEAL ME IF HE WANTS TO

This is one of the main assumptions and it centers around God's willingness to heal.

There are many today who have not received divine healing or some other miracle, because of their inassurance of His willingness. Many of them pray to Him to heal them, and do not get healed because they don't really expect Him to heal them or they're not certain of His will.

" Is God willing to heal me? Will He heal me?"

This is the question in many hearts today. They know they want to be healed. The doctor has given up hope or offers little of it. They're willing to be healed, but they've been told God heals whoever He chooses to, and doesn't even do so all the time. So, they're not sure if they will be among the *lucky* ones to be healed.

Generally, people don't question God's ability to heal them. Their doubts arise when it comes to His willingness to heal them particularly.

However, the Bible clearly lets us

know God's will concerning divine healing.

"And there came a leper to him, beseeching him, and kneeling down to him, and saying unto him, if thou wilt, thou canst make me clean". **(Mark 1:40)**

This man was a leper who came out to Jesus in the city. When he saw Jesus, he bowed and worshipped Him and said, *"Lord, if thou wilt thou canst make me clean".*

Just like many people today, the leper didn't question the Lord's ability. He probably had heard of His many miracles. He probably knew of some other leper who had been healed. Like some today, who are very much aware of their neighbour's testimony of healing from cancer, or asthma, or diabetes, yet they wonder, *'what about me? Yes, I know so and so was healed, but what about me? Will He heal me?'*

Thank God we have His Word to guide us. Thank God we can read the Lord's reply. I always say that Jesus knew He was answering not only the question in the hearts of those who were present then, but that also of many generations to come. Thus, He both demonstrated and verbally affirmed His willingness to heal. *"And Jesus, moved with compassion, put forth His hand, and touched him, and saith unto him, I will; be thou clean"* **(Mark 1:41).**

With much compassion, He stretched forth His hand and touched him even before he was cured, something that no one else would have done for fear of contamination. By that simple touch Jesus demonstrated love, compassion and acceptance to the leper and gave him assurance of His will to heal him, as He replied, *"I WILL: be thou clean"*.

The reply of the Master still applies today, and should allay your fears. He can heal you, but even more importantly, He wants to heal you. This should help you know the mind of God, so you can have the right attitude, perception and understanding of God's Word on this issue, as these will positively influence the effectiveness of your prayers. Believe it's God's will to heal you.

Assumption 2:

GOD WILL HEAL ME WHEN HE CHOOSES TO

There are those who think God would only heal someone when He wants to; and when He doesn't, He wouldn't. They think, 'Whenever God chooses, He will heal me,' but that's not true. It used to be true but it's no longer true.

Let me illustrate it this way. Imagine that I am a student in college and my dad said to me, *"I will send you money once every month".* Then I thanked him and went to school. Throughout that semester, he sent me money monthly, and I lacked nothing. Now that was the way we operated that whole semester.

Then came a new semester and my Dad said to me, *"I have opened an account for you in a bank close to your school and deposited an amount of money in it, having known what it took you to go through the last semester. Whenever you need money, go down to that bank and get it yourself".* Now it's no longer true this semester that he sends me money monthly. That was true last semester but things are different this new semester. Now there is a better system. All the money I would need for this semester has been paid to my account. Understand the difference? That is the same way God operates with us now.

Back in the Old Testament, He said, *"... I will be gracious to whom I will be gracious, and will shew mercy on whom I will shew mercy"* **(Exodus 33:19).** But then He said to Abraham, *"Through your seed shall all the nations of the earth be blessed"* **(Genesis 12:2-3).**

The Bible tells us that Jesus Christ is the Seed of Abraham to whom all the promises were made, and if you belong to Christ then you are Abraham's seed, and an heir according to the promise (Galatians 3: 16,

29).

So now that Christ has come, we are 'the blessed'. God has given us all of the blessings in Him. He doesn't have any more blessings He's holding back from us, and saying, *"Whenever I choose to, I'll give it to you".* No! He has made all the blessings available to us in Christ Jesus.

"Blessed be the God and Father of our Lord Jesus Christ, who hath blessed us with all spiritual blessings in heavenly places in Christ: According as he hath chosen us in him before the foundation of world' that we should be holy and without blame before him in love: Having predestinated us unto the adoption of children by Jesus Christ to himself, according to the good pleasure of his will, To the praise of the glory of his grace, wherein he hath made us accepted in the beloved. In whom we have redemption through his blood, the forgiveness of sins, according to the riches of his grace;" **(Ephesians 1:3-7)**

Notice that he didn't say 'who is going to', but he said 'who hath'. God has already blessed us with all spiritual blessings in heavenly realms. He didn't say, 'with some spiritual blessings', but 'with ALL spiritual blessings in heavenly places in Christ' Your health is just one of those blessings.

Spiritual blessings are actually the greatest. All other blessings come from the spiritual, because the spirit world gave birth to the material world.

The Bible tells us that *"In the beginning God created the heaven and the earth"* **(Genesis 1:1).** God pre-existed the heavens and the earth He created. God is a Spirit (John 4: 4), and if He being a Spirit, created the material and physical world, which He did, then the spirit world in which God dwells must be greater than the material and physical. So, spiritual blessings gave birth to physical and material blessings. This means when God tells us He has blessed us with all spiritual blessings, He has actually given us everything.

You see, in the mind of God, you have been healed already. If you are born again, the Bible says of Jesus, *"...by whose stripes, ye were healed."* **(1 Peter 2: 24).** Peter was referring to Isaiah's prophecy in Isaiah 53. Isaiah in his time looked into the future and saw Jesus giving Himself for the world. Then he declared, *"...with his stripes we are healed."* **(Isaiah 53:5).** Peter, on the other hand, looks back from a New Testament position at what Christ had already done, and affirms, *"...by whose stripes YE WERE HEALED."*

This should correct the wrong assumption that God will heal only when He wants to, because He's already done it. He did it 2000 years ago. So when does God want you healed? *'2000 years ago'*! This should let you know that God has done everything necessary for you to live a healthy, fulfilling life. But it's one thing for God to give, and another for you to receive. Right now, you may not be experiencing the blessing you have desired for so long, but the problem is not with God giving it to you. Just like the illustration I gave of my dad opening an account for me, and depositing all the money I needed to go through the semester, God also has opened for us a joint account with Jesus and has made an all-sufficient, all-time deposit in that account. Everything Jesus has, and every right and privilege that He enjoys, belongs to you today. It is now up to you to make withdrawals on that account as often as you need to.

Assumption 3:

GOD DISCIPLINES HIS CHILDREN WITH SICKNESS

This is a lie from the pit of hell, and a lot of Christians have bought it hook, line and sinker. Quite a number of people, both believers and non-believers, sincerely believe that God inflicts sickness on His children to make them humble. In their religious minds, they think God knew that but for the sickness, some of His children would have lived terrible lives. But the Bible lets us know that *"Every good gift and every perfect gift is from above, and cometh down from the Father of lights, with whom is no variableness, neither shadow of turning."* (James 1:17).

Only good gifts come from our heavenly Father. Sicknesses would hardly qualify as a gift, not to mention being a good or perfect one. Sickness is from the devil and God does not need the devil's tool to fix any good thing for His children. Why would He have to use the instrument of Satan to perform a good deed in your life? If God put sickness on you to humble you, and then you ran to your doctor, or took drugs to take away what God put on you to make you humble, wouldn't that be hypocrisy? The truth is God never inflicts sickness on any of His children to make them humble.

A good father would never like to see his children suffer. Rather, he works hard to ensure they don't. No earthly parent could love or care for his children better than God.

No parent could be more willing to do good things for their family than He. God is the best daddy there is. He is your Father and He wants the very best for you. Recognize and take full advantage of the Fatherhood of God, knowing that His will is to bless and not to curse.

John by the Spirit spoke the heart of God when he said, *"Beloved, I wish above all things that thou mayest prosper and be in health, even as thy soul prospereth."* **(3 John 2).**

This is God's desire for you. He is more willing to heal you than you are ready to be healed. He anointed Jesus with the Holy Ghost and with power, and Jesus went about doing good and healing all that were oppressed of the devil (Acts 10: 38).

Jesus was anointed to bless you. He was anointed to help you get well and live in health. That is what He came to do; to give you abundant life (John 10:10).

God continually proves His willingness to heal people at our teaching and healing crusades. So many people are healed of diverse kinds of sicknesses; across several cities and nations. Christians, Muslims, atheists; all are healed, with some not even expecting to receive a miracle. Glory to God! This is just one simple proof of God's willingness, and eagerness to heal. Now let these truths be settled in your heart forever:

 God can heal you. He has the power to.

 God wants you well.

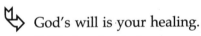 God's will is your healing.

If He has healed so many others before you, then He will heal you too. He paid for your healing in Christ Jesus. What He has done for one, He will do for anyone under the same circumstances. And even if your case is the first ever of its kind, God will meet you at the point of your need. He has healed many such "first cases" before. Remember Jesus Christ is the same yesterday, today and forever!

2

Receive Your Miracle!

God is not choosing whom to bless and whom not to bless. He's not choosing to bless one and curse the other. He has chosen to bless everyone in Christ Jesus. The question now is: How do we tap into what belongs to us? How do we receive and enjoy the blessings that are already ours? How do we receive a miracle without trying to get God to give it, since He already has? You may be in a situation right now where you know what you need is a miracle. You know if anyone can help you, it has to be God. I want you to know that that miracle is close to you now.

Let me begin to show you how to receive a miracle.

"And a certain woman which had an issue of blood twelve years, And had suffered many things of many physicians, and had spent all that she had, and was nothing bettered, but rather grew worse, When she had heard of Jesus, came in the press behind, and touched his garment. For she said, If I may touch but his clothes, I shall be whole. And straightway the fountain of her blood was dried up; and she felt in her body that she was healed of that plague. And Jesus, immediately knowing in himself that virtue had gone out of him, turned him about in the press, and said, Who touched my clothes? And his disciples said unto him, Thou seest the multitude thronging thee, and sayest thou, Who touched me? And he looked round about to see her that had done this thing. But the woman fearing and trembling, knowing what was done in her, came and fell down before him, and told him all the truth. And he said unto her, Daughter, thy faith had made thee whole; go in peace, and be whole of thy plague." **(Mark 5:25-34)**

This is a beautiful story, but it wasn't written for us to admire the power of Jesus or applaud the woman's faith. By following the example of this woman, you will be taking the same sure steps she took towards her miracle, and you will have the same results.

HEAR IT AND BELIEVE!

This woman had suffered a terrible hemorrhage for 12 years, but the process of her change began when she heard of Jesus and believed in His ability to heal her. You must HEAR IT. This is the first step towards your miracle.

*"...faith cometh by hearing and hearing by the WORD of God."***(Romans 10:17)**.

If you don't hear, faith cannot come. Faith is not something you are born with from your mother's womb. You may say

'Well, since I was born, I've never had faith.' But now that you need a miracle, hear the Word of God and believe! That's the only way faith can come to you. God's Word imparts faith to the human spirit. He has made the human spirit with the ability and the capacity to receive the Word of God and develop faith. No matter who you are and what your case is, when you listen to the Word of God and believe it, faith will come to you.

This is the reason we publicise our healing crusades. Some people ask, "Why do you advertise?" We are simply adopting the same strategy that Jesus used to reach people in His day. He organized publicity campaigns to create awareness among the people and inspire them to come receive their healing. At one time, He sent out His twelve disciples to preach the Gospel and heal the sick (Mathew 10: 5-8). Another time He sent seventy disciples to go before Him into every city where He was billed to preach. They went announcing His coming, healing the sick as they did (Luke 10:1-9).

"How then shall they call on him in whom they have not believed? and how shall they believe in him of whom they have not heard? and how shall they hear without a preacher?" (Romans 10:14).

This is why it's so important for the message to be proclaimed loudly enough for people to hear it. There are so many people desperately in need of a miracle, and until they hear of such meetings where the power of God is present to heal them, they may never have faith to be touched by God and receive their healing.

You've got to hear God's Word about your situation. Ask yourself, "What has God said about my case?" When you hear it, you can know the right steps to take. If what His Word says is that He's going to do something about it, then you can ask Him to do it, but if He says He's already done it, there is no use asking Him to do it anymore. What you ought to do is receive what He has already done.

This woman had suffered twelve long years. Some of the doctors who treated her didn't know what to do for her anymore. Others just took advantage of her desperate situation to extort money from her. She had become poor from paying them, and all she had to show for it was her worsened state. She could have thought there was nobody to help her anymore and given up all hope after those twelve years. Then, she heard about Jesus. She heard all the wonderful testimonies about Him, how He was opening blind eyes, unstopping deaf ears, healing the crippled, making the maimed whole again, cleansing the lepers, raising the dead, and she believed. Faith rose up in her. She was on course to receiving a spectacular miracle!

SAY IT!

When you have heard the message and believed, the next thing is to SAY IT.

When she heard of Jesus, she said *'if I may but touch his clothes, I shall be whole.' 'She said it.'* The Bible lets us know that she said this to herself. In Matthew's account of the same story, he says,

"And, behold, a woman, which, was diseased with an issue of blood twelve years came behind him, and touched the hem of his garment: For she said within herself..." **(Mathew 9: 20-21).**

You see, she wasn't talking to anybody in particular, but she said it within herself and convinced herself of it.

She must have told herself, "I don't need that man to lay hands on me, if I can just touch the hem of His garment, I shall be well".

This is what you must do. Voice your faith. Say it with your own mouth, 'I will be healed.' Several times I have asked people at our programmes if they knew they were going to be healed, and some of them said they had actually made up their minds they would be healed that day. They say things like 'I knew that this was my day', 'I came expecting to receive my miracle' Of course, there were those who didn't expect to be healed and still got a miracle. Yes, it does happen like that too, but the surest way to receiving it, and keeping it is through these steps I am sharing with you. Once you hear the word about it and **believe it**, then **proclaim it**, voice your faith. Tell yourself and anybody who cares to listen, what you are going to receive from God.

ACT ON IT, NO MATTER WHAT IT TAKES!

After voicing her faith, the woman with the issue of blood needed to take another crucial step. She had to ACT on what she had believed and affirmed.

Now watch this.

You may have decided what you want to do, but, don't expect that everything would just be easy. This woman whose story has taught us so much also faced a big challenge, but she overcame it. Her condition did not favour what she was about to do. Jesus would hardly be found alone in the streets, but she was determined to touch Him all the same. She had gathered enough information on His itinerary and knew He would be coming through the streets on that day. But when she got out there, she found a large crowd pressing hard upon Jesus from all sides. All she wanted to do was just touch Jesus' clothes, but it didn't turn out as easy as she may have thought. Now you may be thinking, *'What was so difficult in that? All she had to do was force her way through the crowd to where Jesus was'* Let me show you what the law said about an issue of blood, so you can appreciate the enormity of the challenge she had to conquer before she received her miracle.

"And if a woman have an issue, and her issue in her flesh be blood, she shall be put apart seven days: and whosoever toucheth her shall be unclean until the even... And whosoever toucheth her bed shall wash his clothes, and bathe himself in water, and be unclean until the even. And whosoever toucheth anything that she sat upon shall wash his clothes, and bathe himself in water, and be unclean until even. And if it be on her bed, or on anything whereon she sitteth, when he toucheth it, he shall be unclean until the even. And if any man lie with her at all, and her flowers be upon him, he shall be unclean seven days; and all the bed whereon he lieth shall be unclean. And if a woman have an issue of blood, many days out of the time of her separation (menstrual period), or if it run beyond the time of her separation; all the days of the issue of her uncleanness shall be as the days of her separation: she shall be unclean. Every bed whereon she lieth all the days of her issue shall be unto her as the bed of her separa-

tion: and whatsoever she sitteth upon shall be unclean, as the uncleanness of her separation. And whosoever toucheth those things shall be unclean, and wash his clothes and bathe himself in water, and be unclean until the even." **(Leviticus 15: 19-27).**

According to the law, for those twelve years this woman had an issue of blood, she was labeled unclean, and, was an outcast in Israel. For twelve years, she was not allowed to go to the house of God; nobody was supposed to touch her, or her clothes or anything she sat on. If anyone did, they would be unclean and wouldn't be allowed into the house of God to worship. They would have to go have a bath, wash their clothes and remain indoors till evening. And if it happened in the evening, they would have to stay indoors until the evening of the next day! Now imagine such a woman coming out and mingling with a crowd of very religious people.

Let's read some more of what the law said:

"Command the children of Israel, that they put out of the camp every leper, and every one that hath an issue, and whosoever is defiled by the dead: Both male and female shall ye put out, without the camp shall ye put them; that they defile not their camps, in the midst whereof I dwell." **(Numbers 5: 2, 3)**

"Thus shall ye separate the children of Israel from their uncleanness; that they die not in their uncleanness, when they defile my tabernacle that is among them." **(Leviticus 15:31).**

Can you see it now? She stood a great risk of getting herself killed because that was what the law recommended for such an action. She had said to herself, *'I am going to touch Jesus' clothes and be made whole.'* But if she touched Jesus, under the law, Jesus and all those in the crowd that she had made bodily contact with while trying to reach Him (and you can bet there would have been lots of them) would have become un-clean. She could have been stoned to death for doing that. This was good enough reason for her to give up the thought of reaching Jesus, but she didn't let it deter her. She acted on what she had heard and believed.

When you have said it, go ahead and do it. She had said, "If I can just touch his clothes, I shall be whole", then she went. But the odds were against her. It didn't look possible but she went ahead and did it anyway.

Don't just sit where you are and say, *'I know if I go to that place, I shall be healed.'*, or, *'if I do this or that...'* and remain where you are. Get up and do it. Don't let your condition stop you; don't let the circumstances discourage you. Let nothing stop you from receiving your desire.

STEP INTO IT!

Now to the big question; how do you receive a miracle? You have heard the Word and believed it, you have voiced your faith, now it's time to receive.

Let's look in Mark's gospel again, *"She had heard the reports concerning Jesus, and she came up behind Him in the throng and touched His garments, For she kept saying, If I only touch His garments, I shall be restored to health. And immediately her flow of blood was dried up at the source, and [suddenly] she felt in her body that she was healed of her [distressing] ailment."* **(Mark 5: 27-29 - AMP).**

The Bible tells us that her flow of blood dried up, at the source. Now she could have thought to herself that the flow only stopped temporarily. The fact that she had an issue of blood didn't mean she was dripping blood every moment of the day. If this were the case, she would have bled to death in those twelve years. The flow occurred from time to time. So she could have convinced herself that this was one of such times when the flow of blood stopped temporarily. She could have told herself, "Well, right now I am not feeling it, but I better not get too excited just yet. Let me get home and watch it for a while, then I'll know if I'm really healed" No! That's not the way to receive. People have lost their healing that way because they did not accept its reality. They were asking doubtfully, *"Is this true; have I really been healed?"* We must understand that divine healing is spiritual. It must therefore be obtained through spiritual principles.

　　Sometimes, when a miracle takes place, you feel the power of God flowing through you. That feeling is almost indescribable. You just notice that something supernatural is happening within you. At that moment when you feel that power go through you, what you need to do is accept it, because what you are experiencing is the healing power of God. Then you take hold of that healing by faith. When you accept that God has healed you, the healing becomes yours.

For instance, if you are in a meeting where there is a word of knowledge given by the Spirit, and a case is mentioned that is exactly like the one you are in, when you hear it, don't think, "Maybe there's another person like me in this place". Step right into it! Enter into that word that has come concerning your case. Give God thanks for your miracle and begin to do what you could not do before.

Jesus taught us to do that in the Bible.

"And he came to Nazareth where he had been brought up: and as his custom was, he went into the synagogue on the sabbath day, and stood up for to read. And there was delivered unto him the book of the prophet Esaias. And when he had opened the book, he found the place where it was written, The Spirit of the Lord is upon me, for he hath anointed me to preach the gospel to the poor; he hath sent me to heal the broken-hearted, to preach deliverance to the captives and recovering of sight to the blind, to set at

liberty them that are bruised, To preach the acceptable year of the Lord" (Luke 4:16-19)

When Jesus read this scripture, He was actually quoting what Isaiah had said about himself (Isaiah 60: 1-3), but He didn't just stop at reading it out to the hearing of the people in the synagogue that day. He went on to appropriate it to Himself. He said to them, *"This day is this scripture fulfilled in your ears"* (Luke 4:21). What Jesus did was to enter into the Word that had been spoken of Him. Remember He said *"I come (In the volume of the book it is written of me,) to do thy will, O God."* (Hebrews 10:7).

This is the way to receive your miracle.

3

Retain Your Miracle

#1. TELL IT TO KEEP IT!

When you receive your healing, tell it. Don't say, "I want to watch it for some time and be sure it's real". No, tell it immediately! When God heals you, be eager to tell it. This is the way to keep it. You receive it by faith and keep it by telling it.

This is what Jesus did for the woman with the issue of blood. She had received a miracle and was trying to sneak away unnoticed, but He knew she could lose her healing, so He asked, "Who touched me?" He was kind and compassionate to her. He didn't fish her out just because He wanted her to know she could not be hidden. He knew if He let her go away, two or three days later, she would probably be saying, "I thought I was healed but I guess I wasn't."

"And when the woman saw that she was not hid, she came trembling and falling down before him, she declared unto him and before all the people..." **(Luke 8: 47).**

If you don't like to share your testimony publicly, learn from this woman. Telling her testimony was at the risk of her own life because, according to the law she was unclean. And before her healing she had made several people in that crowd unclean while trying to reach the Lord. But she didn't think of telling Him secretly, she declared it before Jesus and all the people!

If someone else had not shared her testimony, it's possible this woman would not have heard. And someone else would hear hers and also have faith. Not sharing your testimony is the wrong attitude. That's not the way to keep a miracle you receive from

God. If you want to keep your miracle then do what Jesus made this woman do.

"And when the woman saw that she was not hid, she came trembling and falling down before him, she declared unto him before all the people for what cause she had touched him and how she was healed immediately." **(Luke 8: 47).**

She told the whole story. She didn't say, "Well, it was something terrible, that's all I can say about it, but thank God, I'm healed now". She didn't hide the details from anybody. She told Jesus and all the people there *"…for what cause she had touched him and how she was healed immediately"*

"And he said unto her, Daughter, be of good comfort: thy faith hath made thee whole, go in peace." **(Luke 8: 48).**

When you share your testimony, you are affirming what God has done in you by faith, and that confirms your healing. That faith restores you to wholeness, which is more than just the healing. When you are made whole, anything and everything that you had lost as a result of a sickness is restored to you.

Also, through your testimony, God's Name is magnified. When that woman testified to the healing power of God, little did she know that so many years and generations later, her testimony would still be producing faith in people. As you tell your testimony, many more lives are blessed as their faith is strengthened to receive their healing. This opens the way for God to do mightier things in your life.

#2. MAINTAIN YOUR HEALING THROUGH A POSITIVE CONFESSION

Constantly make a positive declaration that you have been healed, no matter what you see or feel. Keep talking about your miracle. Keep saying, "I was healed; and if I was healed then, I'm still healed now!" The devil may try to show his face by bringing some symptoms into your body, but you must insist that what you have received from God is still yours.

It's the same for salvation. Keep saying that you are saved. Don't say you are still working on it because you are not. You have received Christ into your life. Maintain that confession. Keep talking about your salvation; keep telling people about your new life in Christ. Don't say anything negative to what you have received. The Lord Jesus Himself said,

"...by thy words thou shall be justified, and by thy words thou shall be condemned." **(Mathew 12:37).**

"For with the heart man believeth unto righteousness, and WITH THE MOUTH CONFESSION IS MADE UNTO SALVATION."

(Romans 10:10).

Confession is speaking the same thing with God. It means that you declare that the same Spirit which raised up Christ from the dead dwells in you and gives life to your body. As you speak God's Word about your body that way, an atmosphere of health remains within and around you. Not only will your general health improve as a result, it will also bring you into God's best for you, which is DIVINE HEALTH.

#3. REJECT NEGATIVE THOUGHTS

Thoughts are very important.
"For as he thinketh in his heart, so is he:..." **(Proverbs 23:7).**

The thoughts that come to your mind and those that you dwell on after you have received your healing will determine whether or not you will keep your healing. Negative thoughts of defeat like, "You are not healed", or "It wouldn't last", come from the devil.

"...Resist the devil, and he will flee from you." **(James 4:7b).**

Reject all negative thoughts. Instead fill your mind with thoughts of life and healing. If you think defeat, you will be defeated; if you think health, you will walk in divine health. Choose health and live in it.

You've got to reject negative thoughts. Don't accept them.

'You were not healed afterall, stop fooling yourself, can't you see that you are feeling the same way as before?' Thoughts like these may sometimes come to you. Such thoughts are not from God, neither are they your thoughts. They are from the devil and that's when you must put your foot down and say,

"No way, I am a child of God, I have received divine health and it's in me now. " You keep insisting on what you've got.

#4. DON'T REGARD SYMP-TOMS

After you have received your miracle, don't expect the devil to go back and fold his hands saying, "Well, I was just trying you with sickness, I'm happy for you now that you are healed". Don't expect him to think that way. He has tried to keep you bound in sickness and has succeeded at it all this while until you received your healing. He wouldn't just let you be and go his way, rejoicing that you have been healed. He's going to put up a fight! He will come back playing every trick he knows to steal that healing from you. He would throw his symptoms at you. That's the devil's chiefest means of a counter-attack.

A symptom is a lying dart of the devil.

It is not the sickness in itself, but a sign of its presence. Symptoms in themselves are not anything, but they point you to something. When you tell a doctor you are sick of something or are feeling certain pains, he starts looking for signs that will point him to what the sickness is. If, for instance, you want to go to a Church you've never been before, you look out for the signboard of the Church that will point you to where it is. You will be kidding to find that sign and stay by it and tell yourself, "Yes, I'm now in Church". You have not arrived there yet. The signboard is not the Church; it merely points you to where the Church is.

The devil knows how to play tricks with signs. He may put them all around your body, one in your eye, another in your leg or in your head, and all those symptoms seem to point to the return of that sickness. The moment you say, "Oh, I've got the sickness", that's when the devil really gets you, because the sickness actually comes from your words, not from the signs.

Those symptoms are just like a mirage. So you must refuse to acknowledge them when they come. In fact you can laugh at the devil and tell him, "Devil, you are a loser, I know you are lying with all of your symptoms, now get out of here, leave my body in Jesus' Name!" Shake that thing off in the Name of Jesus!

Don't be afraid of symptoms. When you feel one, don't say,

"That's the way I used to feel when that sickness was on me". That's just a feeling and we walk by faith, not by sensory perception (2 Corinthians 5: 7).

Did you ever hear that Jesus cursed a fig tree? He said to the fig tree, *"...No man eat fruit of thee hereafter for ever..."***(Mark 11: 14).** The disciples saw Jesus talking to the tree and they heard what He said, but the tree looked just the same as they went on their way. But the Bible says,

"And in the morning, as they passed by,

*they saw the fig tree dried up from the roots.
And Peter calling to remembrance, saith unto
him, Master, behold the fig tree which thou
cursedst is withered away. And Jesus answering saith unto them, Have faith in God."*
(Mark 11: 20-22)

Every tree receives life from its roots;
so that's the right place to curse it. Jesus
cursed that tree but it looked the same though
it was dead from the roots. When a sickness
is rebuked or commanded to die, it dies from
its roots, the very life of it. You may still feel
some pain, the swelling may still look like it's
there, but the life of it is gone. Its source has
been destroyed and it cannot continue. It's just
the same as when you switch off a fan. For a
few moments the blades still rotate, but it cannot continue because it's been cut off from its
source of current.

You are the only one that can make
that sickness return by saying, *'I thought I was
healed, but I don't think so any more'* So don't
say that; rather, say, *'That sickness has*

been *cursed to die and it remains dead!'*

The Bible tells us, *"They that observe lying vanities forsake their own mercy."* **(Jonah 2:8).** Your health is your mercy, don't forsake it by observing symptoms for they are lying vanities.

Remember, you are not healed because you don't feel the pains any more, but because God's Word declares *"...by whose (Jesus') stripes ye were healed"* **(1 Peter 2: 24).**

#5. KEEP EXERCISING YOUR FAITH

You exercise your faith by acting your believing. Whatever you couldn't do before because of that sickness, you can do now that you are healed and keep at it. Don't say, *'I tried to walk and fell down, so decided never to try again.'*

No. Don't give up. Keep doing it.

You must insist to your body what it should do.

When you were born, you were 'lame'. You may never have heard it this way before, but think about it, and you will agree it's true. You didn't start walking all over the place the moment you came out of your mother's womb. You were actually lame when you came out because you couldn't walk. If you were born among people that never walked or were never taught to walk, you probably would never have walked in your life. Somebody had to teach you and help you: you watched other people who were walking and you began to act like them and they taught you to walk.

When you receive a miracle, keep acting the faith that brought you that miracle in the first place. Keep acting your believing, keep doing it. If you can take four steps today, try five tomorrow. Just keep doing it and while you're doing it, you say, '*I am walking in the Name of Jesus, the strength of God is in me. I can do all things through Christ that energizes me'*

#6. ABSTAIN FROM SIN AND STAY IN THE RIGHT ENVIRONMENT

As a child of God you've been called out of the world. Don't go back to sin. Sin is the devil's tool for bringing people into bondage and death. *"For the wages of sin is death;..."* **(Romans 6: 23).** You may ask, "What if I sin?" If you do, God will forgive you, but don't deliberately go back to sin. Don't make a habit of sinning.

Jesus said to the man He healed at the pool of Bethesda, *"...See, you are well! Stop sinning or something worse may happen to you."* **(John 5:14 Amplified Translation).**

This lets you know that living an unholy life can lead you into a condition even worse than the one you were healed from. But by being in the right environment, you can establish your dominion over sin and live a godly life. The Bible instructs in Proverbs 1: 10, "If sinners entice thee, consent thou not" and also tells us that evil communication corrupts good manners (1 Corinthians 15:33). So don't move among the wrong folk. Get among God's people. In the Kingdom, we have a different kind of behaviour and language. There are things we just don't say or do as Christians. They are too dirty for us to be involved with. If you go back to the world, where they talk, act and think dirty, you're going to live that way again and give the devil an opening in your life. So *"...come out from among them, and be ye separate..."* **(2 Corinthians 6:17).**

If you don't have Christian friends, it's time to make some. You don't even have to tell your old friends off. Just make new ones among Christians and the old ones will either come along with you into Christ, or stay away from you. You just wouldn't see them again. Those who will come to you will do so because they believe your testimony.

#7. ATTEND CHURCH MEETINGS REGULARLY

This is also very important, because in the Church, the Holy Spirit ministers to His children. Being in God's presence can be likened to the sun. Everybody receives from it whatever they want. Some want heat, some want light, others want some other energy. Whatever it is they want, the sun shines and they all receive from it. Now, when you come into the Church, the Spirit of God answers your questions and brings thoughts to your mind. Sometimes you may not immediately need those thoughts, but sooner or later they become relevant and applicable to your life.

Do you know that you really do not see a blessing with your optical eyes? You only see the results. The Holy Spirit blesses you when you are in the Church. This is why you must regularly attend Church services, don't miss them. The teaching, the praise, worship, and prayers all serve to communicate the presence of God and something always happens where God's presence is; where the Holy Spirit is working.

"Behold, how good and how pleasant it is for brethren to dwell together in unity!.. for there the LORD commanded the blessing, even life forever more."(Psalm 133:1,3).

Then He also cleanses you as you listen to the Word in Church. God's Word purifies your heart. The wrong thoughts leave you and all the stains of sin in your life are stripped away. The Holy Spirit washes your spirit clean with the Word (Titus 3: 5; Ephesians 5: 26), and by the time you are getting up to leave Church, you have become so pure in your heart and ready to face the world again.

#8. PRAY ALWAYS

You also have to pray regularly because

prayer helps you keep communication with your Heavenly Father through the Holy Spirit.

The Bible instructs us to pray always. Paul by the Spirit in 1 Thessalonians 5: 17 instructs, "Pray without ceasing." This is an essential part of developing your relationship with God. It keeps you in His Word and creates a conducive atmosphere for you to exercise your faith, and maintain that atmosphere of positivity and faith around yourself. It gets you attuned to the power of God within you.

Prayer is a weapon against the attacks of the devil.

Ephesians 6: 18 says, *"Praying always with all prayer and supplication in the Spirit, and watching thereunto with all perseverance and supplication for all saints;"*

PRAY IN THE SPIRIT ALWAYS, GIVING YOURSELF
TO PRAYER JUST LIKE JESUS DID.

#9. STUDY THE WORD

Let me tell you this: if there is anything you should know in this life, it is the
word of God. Learn God's Word for yourself
through the help of the Holy Spirit. Crave
the Word, go for it more than anything in this
whole wide world.

It's only through the Word you can
know that God's will is for you to live in divine health, or else the devil will keep you in
sickness or even kill you. By studying God's
Word, your mind becomes renewed, then you
begin to think and talk like God.

*"We having the same spirit of faith, accord-
ing as it written, I believed, and therefore have
I spoken; we also believe, and therefore
speak;"***(2 Corinthians 4:13).**

Get acquainted with all of God's will
through the word. Spend quality time studying God's Word so you can be adequately in-
formed. You may ask, *'What are the things I*

should read, where do I begin?'

John's Gospel and the Book of Ephesians are some portions that will inspire you. By the time you are through studying them, you would always want to be with your Bible. Study them carefully. Don't just rush through them one morning and say you have finished studying. As you study John's gospel, discover for yourself what the Master said. Now don't you go and get a red-letter edition and say you have discovered them already. Get to find out what He actually said and in their right context.

Find out everything the book of Ephesians says, each time you read "In Christ", "In Him" or "in whom". Find out everything He says He has already done, everything in the past tense that concerns the Church, what He says about your position, and what He says belongs to you.

When you study these truths, you will develop an insatiable desire for God's Word, because, you will discover so much about God, and about yourself that will become real in your life. And you will never want to leave your Bible again.

"Let the word of God dwell in you richly in all wisdom; teaching and admonishing one another in psalms and hymns and spiritual songs, singing with grace in your hearts to the Lord."(Colossians 3:16).

THE WORD OF GOD IS A MEDICINE THAT WILL KEEP YOU ALWAYS IN HEALTH.

"My son, attend to my words; incline thine ear unto my sayings. Let them not depart from thine eyes; keep them in the midst of thine heart. For they are life unto those that find them, and health to all their flesh." (Proverbs 4:20-22).

Beloved, commit yourself to the Word of God and meditate continually on it. It will bring health and joy to you. It will become a compelling power inside you that keeps you living the victorious life.

*To know more about
the ministry and messages of
Pastor Chris Oyakhilome
Contact:*

CHRIST EMBASSY
aka Believers' LoveWorld Inc.

LONDON ADDRESS:
*Christ Embassy Int'l Office
Suite 219 Estuary House
Ballards Road
Dagenham RM10 9AB*

*P.O. Box 21520
London E10 5FG
Tel/Fax: -208-5172367*

NIGERIA ADDRESS:
*P.O. Box 13563,Ikeja,
Lagos, Nigeria.
Tel: 01-4934392-3; 7740109; 7740243*

*email: cec@christembassy.org
website:www.christembassy.org*

None Of These Diseases

There is yet to be a more comprehensive and insightful teaching on the subject of divine healing and health. Certainly, the sick will be healed and raised up when they discover the truths contained in this timely release by Pastor Chris. The healed will see and understand why and how to stay in divine health.

You will receive faith for your miracle and begin to enjoy the fullness of life which God has provided for you.

This book will stir in and around you an atmosphere for miracles!

The Promised Land

Chris Oyakhilome

The Promised Land is a classic expose on the Christian life. It offers Bible based answers to a lot of questions, and provides explanation needed to live a constantly victorious life.

You need to read about the promise, war in the Promised Land, a kingdom of priests; all in The Promised Land. Every page is filled with divine truths. You will need to read The Promised Land again, and again.

It is a must for every Christian, every minister, and every serious student of the Bible.

The Oil And The Mantle

"The Oil & The Mantle" exposes the myth about the use of material mediums to perform miracles and reveals clearly the mind of God on the subject.

An explicit treatise, it will change your thinking on these controversial issues, and cause you to be established in the truth.